- 4 Fastest fixed-wing craft
- 5 Fastest military aircraft
- 6 Fastest bomber
- 7 Fastest airliner
- 8 Fastest helicopter
- 9 Biggest airship
- 10 Biggest airliner
- 12 Biggest aircraft

record breakers

- 13 Heaviest bomber
- 14 Longest wingspan
- 15 Longest flight
- 16 First transatlantic flight
- 17 First jet aircraft
- 18 First jet airliner
- 19 First supersonic aircraft
- 20 First round-the-world flight
- 21 Biggest cargo hold
- 22 Least detectable aircraft
- 23 Busiest airport
- 24 Longest human-powered flight

Text, illustration and design © 1997 The Templar Company plc.

SKY *file*

The Lockheed SR-71 'Blackbird' spy-plane holds the world air speed record. In July 1976, a Blackbird reached a speed of 3,529.56 km/h - that's more than three times the speed of sound. The Blackbird's job was to fly so high and so fast over enemy countries that it could spy on them without any danger of being attacked.

Lockheed SR-71 Blackbird

fastest aircraft

Hot stuff

If most aircraft were fitted with powerful enough engines to fly as fast as the Blackbird, their aluminium body would melt! Air rubbing against a plane flying at mach 3 heats parts of it to more than 500 degrees Celsius. The Blackbird is made from titanium, which does not melt until it reaches 1,660 degrees.

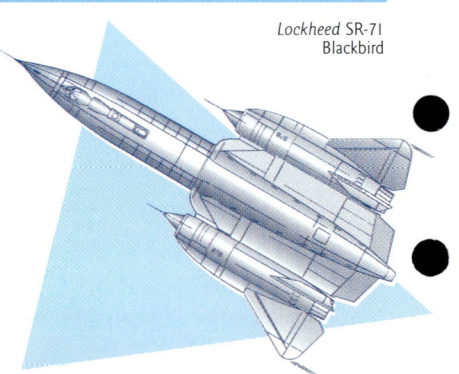

Lockheed SR-71 Blackbird

F A C T

The speed of sound is also known as mach 1. Twice the speed of sound is mach 2 and three times the speed of sound is mach 3.

fastest air-launched aircraft

SKY *file*

FACT
The X-15 was 15 metres long with a wing-span of only 6.7 metres. It weighed 15,000 kilograms.

To hold the world air speed record, an aircraft has to take off from the ground and land again under its own power. There are faster aircraft, but they do not take off under their own power. They are launched from another aircraft. The fastest of these is the X-15 rocket-plane. It was a fuel tank with a cockpit at one end and a rocket engine at the other end.

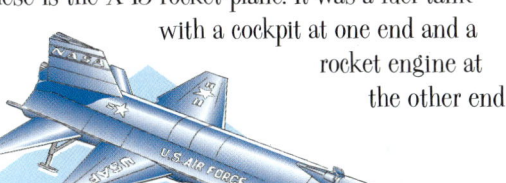

X-15

Three .. two .. one ... launch

The X-15 was carried up into the sky underneath the wing of a B-52 bomber. At a height of almost 14,000 metres, it was released from the B-52. The pilot would then light the X-15's rocket engine and soar to a height of up to 100,000 metres and a speed of up to 7,300 km/h - that's nearly seven times the speed of sound.

SKY file

The fastest craft of any sort with wings is the US Space Shuttle. When it re-enters the Earth's atmosphere at the end of a space mission, it is flying at the incredible speed of more than 28,000 km/h - about 25 times the speed of sound. Its wings are short and stubby because long thin wings would be burned off during re-entry.

> **FACT**
> Flying into the atmosphere at 25 times the speed of sound heats up the Space Shuttle so much that it has to be covered with thousands of glassy tiles to protect it from the heat.

fastest fixed-wing craft

Gliding home

The Space Shuttle is blasted into space by amazingly powerful rocket engines, but it returns to Earth like a glider. It flies down through the atmosphere from space without any engine power at all, so its crew has only one chance to get the landing right.

Space Shuttle

fastest military aircraft

SKY *file*

An interceptor is a type of fighter plane that is designed to fly as fast as possible. Its job is to meet approaching enemy aircraft and stop them before they can do any damage. The fastest military interceptor is the Russian MiG-25. It has a top speed of about 3,400 km/h, three times the speed of sound.

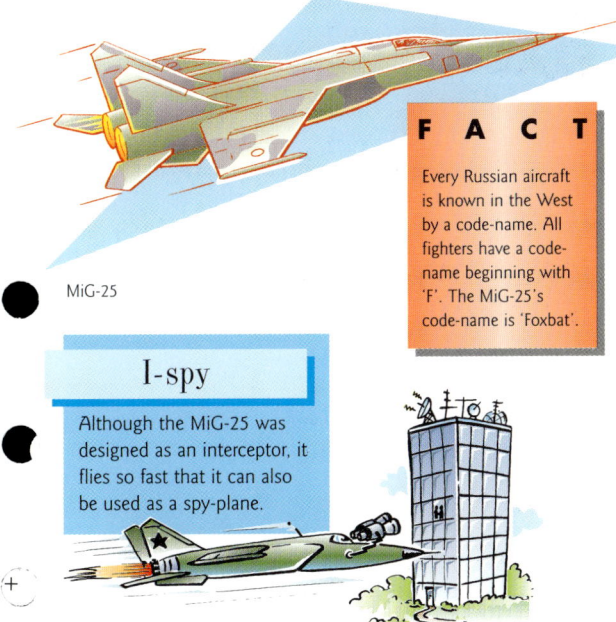

MiG-25

F A C T

Every Russian aircraft is known in the West by a code-name. All fighters have a code-name beginning with 'F'. The MiG-25's code-name is 'Foxbat'.

I-spy

Although the MiG-25 was designed as an interceptor, it flies so fast that it can also be used as a spy-plane.

SKY file

General Dynamics F-111

fastest bomber

During both world wars, bombers were bigger and slower than fighters. The size and weight of the bombs they had to carry slowed them down. But nowadays there are several supersonic bombers that fly faster than many fighters. The fastest is the American General Dynamics F-111, which has a maximum speed of about 2,655 km/h, or just over $2\frac{1}{2}$ times the speed of sound.

FACT

The F-111 is a swing-wing aircraft. Its wings can swivel backwards to enable it to fly faster.

Multi-purpose planes

Modern military aircraft are so expensive to produce that many of them have to do more than one job. Fighter-bombers try to combine the speed and agility of a fighter with the bomber's ability to drop bombs. The fastest is the McDonnell-Douglas F-15E Eagle, which, like the F-111, can reach a top speed of 2,655 km/h.

General Dynamics F-111

fastest airliner

The world's fastest airliner is the Aerospatiale/BAC Concorde. It is also the world's only supersonic airliner. The slender white dart-shaped plane can cruise at more than twice the speed of sound. Concorde first flew in 1969, the same year as the first Jumbo Jet, and entered service with Air France and British Airways in 1976.

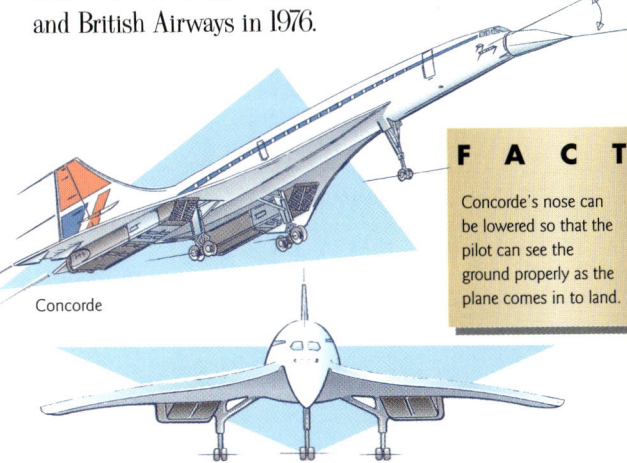

Concorde

F A C T

Concorde's nose can be lowered so that the pilot can see the ground properly as the plane comes in to land.

Hot stuff

Air rushing past Concorde as it hurtles through the atmosphere heats part of it to a temperature of 127 degrees Celsius. When metal heats up it expands. Concorde actually grows 15 centimetres longer during a flight than it is when it is sitting on the ground.

SKY file

Helicopters cannot fly as fast as fixed-wing aircraft. Their whirling rotor blades cannot slip through the air as easily as fixed wings and a lot of their engine power goes into creating lift instead of propelling the aircraft forwards. So, the fastest helicopters are slower than the fastest fixed-wing aeroplanes. The fastest helicopter is a Westland Lynx, which reached a speed of 400.87 km/h in August 1986.

FACT
Most helicopters are powered by a type of jet engine called a turbo-shaft.

Westland Lynx

fastest helicopter

Tiltrotor

A new type of aircraft called a Tiltrotor combines the ability to take-off vertically like a helicopter with the higher flying speeds of a fixed-wing plane. Rotor blades over each wing lift a Tiltrotor straight up into the air. The engines and rotors swivel forwards and it flies like a normal fixed-wing plane.

Tiltrotor

biggest
airship

Airships built in Germany at the beginning of the 20th century by Count Ferdinand von Zeppelin grew steadily bigger and bigger until the biggest of them all, the Hindenburg, was built in 1936. It was 245 metres long and 41 metres across.

F A C T

The Hindenburg's four engines pushed it along at 125 km/h, just below its top speed of 135 km/h. It took 3.5 days for the Hindenburg to make its regular transatlantic journey from Frankfurt, Germany to New York, USA.

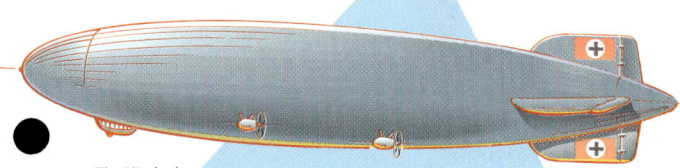

The Hindenburg

A London Bus at the same scale

Lift

The hydrogen gas inside the Hindenburg could lift a total of 244 tonnes. The airship itself weighed 132 tonnes and the fuel needed for a transatlantic flight weighed about 65 tonnes, leaving 47 tonnes for the crew, up to 70 passengers and their baggage.

SKY file

Fuel tanks

An airliner's wings look thin, but they actually contain tanks that hold most of the plane's fuel. A Jumbo Jet's wing tanks are huge. A 747-400 can carry up to 163 tonnes of fuel.

biggest
airliner

Boeing 747-400

FACT

Jumbo Jets are double-deckers. First class passengers fly in an upper deck housed inside a bulge at the front of the plane.

The world's biggest airliner is the Boeing 747-400 Jumbo Jet. The first Jumbo Jet, the 747-100, quickly became the world's standard airliner for the longest flights. New versions were built, bigger and heavier each time. The latest and biggest, the 747-400, is 71 metres from nose to tail and 64 metres from wing-tip to wing-tip. It can carry up to 568 passengers and weighs up to 395 tonnes at take-off.

SKY *file*

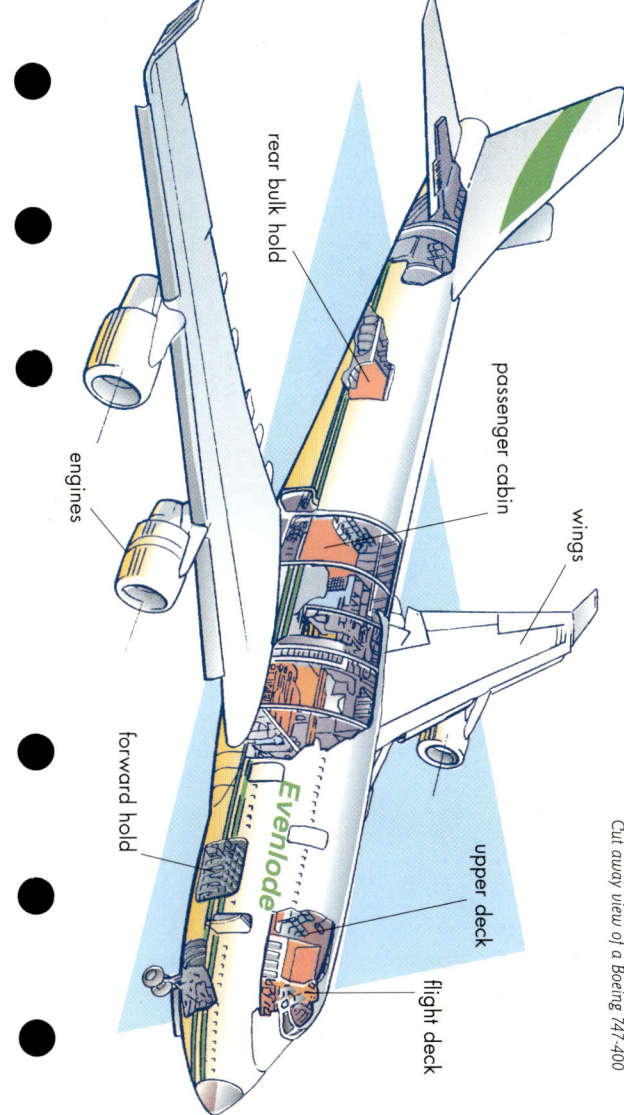

Cut away view of a Boeing 747-400

The Boeing 747-400 Jumbo Jet may be the world's biggest airliner, but there are even bigger aircraft. Military cargo aircraft have to be big to carry the large loads that they have to transport. The largest is the Russian Antonov An-225 Mriya (Dream). It is also the world's heaviest aircraft, with a maximum take-off weight of 600 tonnes.

biggest aircraft

Antonov An-225

F A C T

Only one An-225 has ever been built, by converting an Antonov An-124 Condor transport plane, which is itself the world's largest production aircraft.

Piggy-back passenger

The An-225 was built to transport the Russian Space Shuttle. The Shuttle craft is too big to fit inside the plane, so it sits on top of the An-225's back. The plane had to be specially strengthened to carry the spacecraft safely.

SKY *file*

• heaviest bomber

The world's heaviest bomber is the Russian Tupolev Tu-160. It is also the world's largest bomber and the heaviest combat aircraft ever built. It measures 54 metres from nose to tail, has a wing-span of 56 metres and can weigh up to 275 tonnes.

Swing-wing

The Tu-160 is a swing-wing plane. As it accelerates to its cruising speed of 850 km/h, its wings swivel backwards so that it can slip through the air more easily. It cruises just below the speed of sound, but if necessary it can swivel its wings all the way back and accelerate to a speed of 2,000 km/h, almost twice the speed of sound.

Tupolev Tu-160 Blackjack

F A C T

Russian bombers are known in the West by code-names beginning with 'B'. The Tu-160's code-name is Blackjack.

SKY file

longest
wingspan

Aircraft have been getting bigger and bigger since the Wright Flyer made the first ever powered flight in 1903, so you might expect the plane with the longest wing-span to be one of the most modern planes. In fact, the record-breaking wing-span belongs to the Hughes H4 Hercules flying boat, which was built in 1947. It measured 97.51 metres from wing-tip to wing-tip.

FACT

The Hughes H4 Hercules was built from wood, so it was nicknamed the 'Spruce Goose'

Hughes H4 Hercules 'Spruce Goose'

Maiden flight

The Spruce Goose's maiden (first) flight was also its last. On November 2nd 1947, it skimmed the waves at Long Beach Harbour in California, USA, and splashed down again after 914 metres. At the beginning of the Jet Age it was already out of date by the time it made its first flight.

SKY *file*

The longest non-stop scheduled flight, a flight you can buy a ticket for, is between New York, USA, and Johannesburg, South Africa, a distance of 12,823 kilometres.

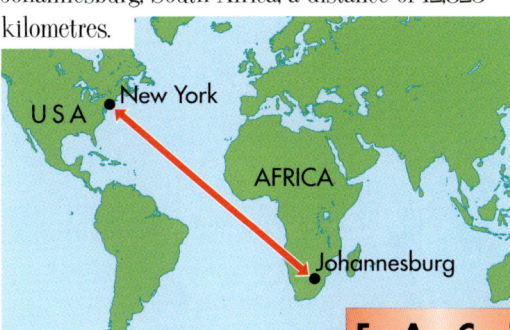

longest flight

F A C T

Airliners can fly incredibly long distances now compared to the first airliners. The Empire flying boats that carried passengers between England and Africa, India and the Far East in the 1930s had to land every 1,200 kilometres at most.

Non-schedule

Airliners have flown further than the New York to Johannesburg flight, although not in regular passenger service. In June 1993, an Airbus A340-200 airliner flew non-stop halfway round the world, from Auckland, New Zealand to Paris, France, a distance of 18,545 kilometres.

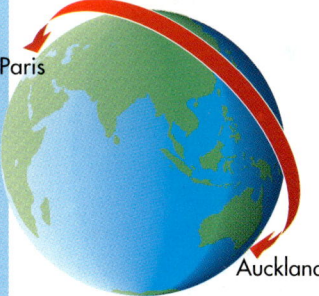

SKY file

Special planes

Special flights need special aircraft. Lindbergh made his historic solo transatlantic flight in a converted Ryan NYP. It took two months to convert the aircraft. Fuel tanks filled most of the front half of the plane. Lindbergh had to use a periscope to look round the tanks and see where he was going.

first transatlantic flight

Alcock and Brown's Vickers Vimy

FACT

The first solo non-stop transatlantic flight was made by Charles Lindbergh in May 1927 in his aircraft called Spirit of St Louis.

Aircraft did not cross the Atlantic Ocean until 1919. A US Navy Curtiss NC-4 Seaplane piloted by Lieutenant-Commander Albert Cushion Read and his crew survived dreadful weather to cross from Newfoundland, Canada, to Lisbon, Portugal, with a re-fuelling stop in the Azores. Only 18 days later, Alcock and Brown made the first non-stop transatlantic flight in a Vickers Vimy bomber.

first
jet aircraft

Although the jet engine was invented in Britain, the first aircraft to take-off and fly using jet power alone was a German Heinkel He-178. It made its historic flight on August 27th 1939. The flight lasted for only six minutes and the plane reached a speed of 600 km/h. Germany quickly went on to produce the first jet fighter, the Messerschmitt Me-262.

F A C T

The jet engine was invented by Sir Frank Whittle, a young Royal Air Force officer. He tested the first jet engine in 1937.

Heinkel He-178

The Jet Age

The Jet Age began with the German Messerschmitt Me-262 and British Meteor jet-fighters. They both entered the Second World War in 1944, too late to make much difference to the progress of the war. The Me-262 had a top speed of 870 km/h, although one version managed a speed of 1,004 km/h.

SKY file

first
jet airliner

The first jet airliner was the de Havilland Comet. It carried its first passengers from London to Johannesburg, South Africa, on May 2nd 1952. The Comet flew much higher than other airliners. Its ability to fly over the top of storms was very popular with passengers. Its cruising speed of around 790 km/h and range (2,800 kilometres) halved the time for the longest flights.

FACT

The Comet was powered by four de Havilland Ghost jet engines fitted inside the wings.

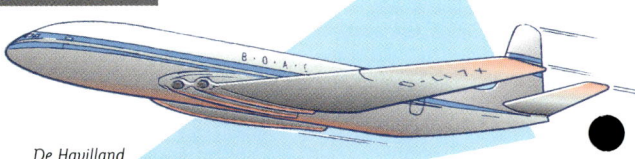

De Havilland Comet

The first jet flight simulator

Nowadays, pilots spend a lot of time training in flight simulators. The world's first jet flight simulator was built to train Comet pilots how to fly the world's first jet airliner. As the crew moved the controls, the cockpit moved and the instruments behaved as if it was really flying.

SKY file

Supersonic pilot

The world's first supersonic pilot was Charles 'Chuck' Yeager of the United States Air Force. He made the first supersonic flight in the Bell X-1 experimental rocket-plane with two broken ribs he had suffered in a riding accident.

first supersonic aircraft

Bell X-1

The first supersonic (faster than sound) flight took place on October 14th 1947. The aircraft was the Bell X-1, a small orange plane shaped like a bullet. It was carried in the bomb bay of a Boeing B-29 Superfortress bomber. At a height of 7,600 metres, the B-29 dropped the X-1. Then the X-1 pilot lit the rocket engine and accelerated to the speed of sound and beyond.

F A C T

The speed of sound at the Earth's surface is about 1,225 km/h. In the colder air higher up where aircraft fly, sound travels more slowly, about 1,062 km/h.

first round-the-world flight

The first round-the-world flight was made by two Douglas World Cruiser seaplanes in 1924. They set out from Seattle, Washington, USA, on April 6th and returned 175 days later on September 28th. They had covered a distance of 44,340 kilometres with 72 stops on the way and spent a total of 371 hours in the air.

FACT

The first solo round-the-world flight was made by Wiley Post in his Lockheed Vega plane called Winnie Mae between July 15th and 22nd 1933.

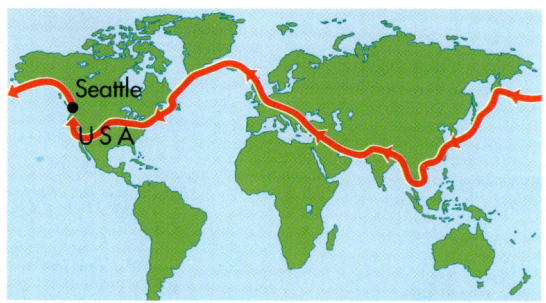

The route of the first round-the-world flight

Non-stop Voyager

On December 14th 1986, Jeana Yeager and Dick Rutan took off from the Edwards Air Force Base in California, USA, in their specially built plane called Voyager. Nine days later they landed where they had started, having made the first non-stop round-the-world flight without landing or re-fuelling on the way.

SKY *file*

Parts of Airbus airliners are made in different European countries. They have to be moved to the assembly points where the planes are put together. They are flown inside a strange-looking aircraft with the world's biggest cargo hold. The A300-600ST was built by Airbus by converting their own A300 airliner. They gave it a huge cargo hold 38 metres long and 7.4 metres across.

F A C T

The A300-600ST is nicknamed the Beluga after a type of whale.

biggest
cargo hold

Airbus A300-600 ST

Super Guppies

Before the A300-600ST Belugas were built, airliner parts were transported around Europe by a fleet of Super Guppy planes that were almost as big as the Beluga. The Super Guppies were built in the 1960s to transport rockets for NASA, the US space agency.

Super Guppy

SKY *file*

Military aircraft are so fast and their weapons so destructive that it is vital to spot them as early as possible so that they can be stopped. A military aircraft that could not be detected would have a better chance of reaching its target and attacking. Stealth aircraft are designed to be difficult to detect. The least detectable aircraft is the Lockheed F-117 Stealth Fighter, or Nighthawk.

F A C T

The Lockheed Nighthawk is 20 metres long, with a wing-span of 13 metres.

least detectable aircraft

Lockheed Stealth Fighter F-117

Skunk Works

The Nighthawk was designed by a secret team at Lockheed called the Skunk Works which specialises in designing the most advanced military aircraft. The Skunk Works designers produced the SR-71 Blackbird spy-plane, the world's fastest plane.

SKY *file*

The first airports were tents or wooden buildings next to a grass landing strip. Nowadays, a major airport is as big as a town, with aircraft taking off and landing every few seconds. The busiest airport in the world is O'Hare International Airport near Chicago, USA. In 1995, more than 67 million passengers travelled to or from O'Hare and there were almost a million aircraft movements (take-offs or landings).

FACT

In 1970, during the Vietnam war, the Ben Hoa Air Base in South Vietnam became the world's busiest landing area, with just over a million take-offs and landings in the year.

busiest airport

International leader

Heathrow Airport, to the west of London, is the fourth busiest airport in the world, but more international passengers pass through Heathrow than any other airport - more than 46 million in 1995.

SKY file

longest human-powered flight

Daedalus '88

Aircraft are normally powered by engines, but specially designed aircraft can be flown by human muscle power. If the plane is light enough, a very fit pilot can pedal hard enough to spin a propeller fast enough to take off. The longest human-powered flight was 119 kilometres, between the islands of Crete and Santorini in the Mediterranean Sea on April 23rd 1988. The pilot was Kanellos Kanellopoulos.

FACT

The Daedalus plane was made from the lightest materials. The whole aircraft weighed only 32 kilograms.

Channel crossing

On June 12th 1979, Bryan Allen made the first human-powered aircraft flight across the English Channel from England to France. The flight took two hours and 49 minutes and covered a distance of 36 kilometres. The plane, called Gossamer Albatross, was designed by Dr Paul MacCready.